THIS BOOK BELONGS TO

_____

FOR THE KIDS WHO WANT TO
BEFRIEND A DRAGON

ISBN: 9798894581859

DEEP IN THE WHISPERING WOODS, A MOUNTAIN WITH A HIDDEN CAVE HELD A SECRET—A MAGICAL LIBRARY GUARDED BY A DRAGON NAMED DRACO.

DRACO, A LARGE, KIND DRAGON WITH SHIMMERING GREEN SCALES,
LOVED BOOKS MORE THAN TREASURE. "EVERY STORY IS A TREASURE,"
HE OFTEN SAID.

ONE EVENING, ELLIE, A CURIOUS GIRL WITH CURLY BROWN HAIR AND WIDE BLUE EYES, WANDERED TOO FAR FROM HER VILLAGE WHILE CHASING FIREFLIES.

THE FIREFLIES LED ELLIE TO THE MOUNTAIN. SHE CLIMBED CAREFULLY, HER BOOTS CRUNCHING AGAINST LOOSE ROCKS.

INSIDE THE CAVE, ELLIE'S MOUTH FELL OPEN. BOOKSHELVES STRETCHED
TO THE CEILING, GLOWING SOFTLY UNDER FLOATING LANTERNS.

DRACO APPEARED, HIS WINGS BLOCKING THE LIGHT.
"WHO DARES ENTER MY LIBRARY?" HE BELLOWED, HIS VOICE ECHOING.

ELLIE GASPED BUT STOOD HER GROUND. "I... I DIDN'T MEAN TO! I JUST...
LOVE BOOKS," SHE STAMMERED.
DRACO'S EYES NARROWED, THEN SOFTENED. "YOU LOVE BOOKS?"

"YES!" ELLIE SAID EAGERLY. "I READ EVERY NIGHT. STORIES ARE MAGICAL!"
DRACO TILTED HIS HEAD. "PERHAPS YOU'RE NOT A THIEF AFTER ALL."

ELLIE STEPPED CLOSER. "THIS LIBRARY IS AMAZING. HOW DID YOU FIND ALL THESE BOOKS?"

"THEY WERE ENTRUSTED TO ME TO PROTECT," DRACO EXPLAINED. "BUT FEW KNOW ABOUT THIS PLACE."

AS THEY TALKED, THE AIR TURNED COLD. DRACO'S EARS TWITCHED. "SOMEONE IS COMING," HE WARNED.

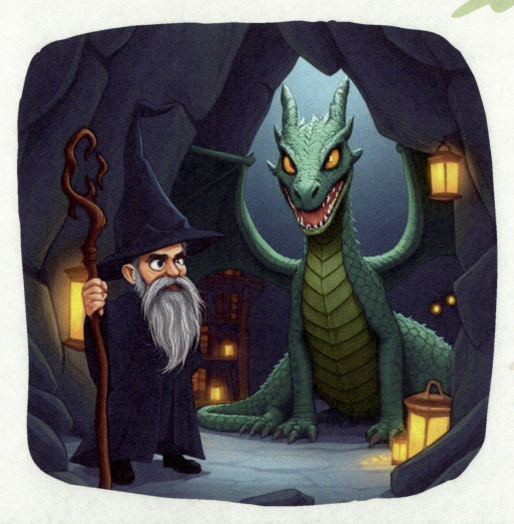

MALGORN, A CLOAKED WIZARD WITH A CROOKED STAFF, APPEARED AT THE ENTRANCE. "AH, DRACO," HE SNEERED. "STILL HOARDING SECRETS?"

DRACO GROWLED. "THIS LIBRARY ISN'T YOURS, MALGORN."
"BUT ITS POWER COULD BE MINE," MALGORN SAID,
HIS STAFF GLOWING OMINOUSLY.

ELLIE HID BEHIND A STACK OF BOOKS AS THE TWO FACED OFF.
"WHAT DOES HE WANT?" SHE WHISPERED TO HERSELF.

MALGORN RAISED HIS STAFF. "STEP ASIDE, DRAGON. YOU CAN'T STOP ME!"
DRACO FLARED HIS WINGS. "WE'LL SEE ABOUT THAT."

A FLASH OF BLUE LIGHT ERUPTED AS MALGORN STRUCK,
SENDING BOOKS FLYING. DRACO ROARED, HIS TAIL WHIPPING THROUGH THE AIR.

DRACO BREATHED FIRE, BUT MALGORN DEFLECTED IT WITH A GLOWING SHIELD. "YOU'RE STRONG, BUT I'M SMARTER!" THE WIZARD CACKLED.

ELLIE SPOTTED A STRANGE BOOK GLOWING ON A HIGH SHELF.
"THAT MIGHT BE IMPORTANT," SHE WHISPERED, CLIMBING UP CAREFULLY.

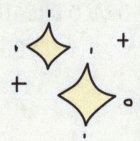

THE BATTLE RAGED BELOW AS ELLIE REACHED THE BOOK. THE COVER
WAS ENGRAVED WITH GOLDEN RUNES AND PULSED WITH WARMTH.

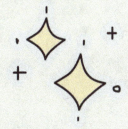

DRACO ROARED, SLAMMING HIS TAIL INTO THE GROUND. THE CAVE SHOOK, AND ELLIE LOST HER BALANCE, TUMBLING DOWN WITH THE BOOK.

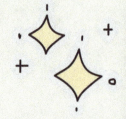

MALGORN TURNED, HIS EYES GLEAMING. "THAT'S THE KEY TO
THE LIBRARY'S MAGIC!"
DRACO GROWLED PROTECTIVELY, STEPPING BETWEEN ELLIE AND THE WIZARD.

"HAND IT OVER, GIRL," MALGORN HISSED, REACHING FOR ELLIE.
"NO!" SHE SHOUTED, CLUTCHING THE BOOK TIGHTLY.

DRACO FLAPPED HIS WINGS, CREATING A GUST THAT KNOCKED MALGORN BACK. "RUN, ELLIE! TAKE THE BOOK TO SAFETY!"

ELLIE NODDED, DARTING THROUGH THE SHELVES. SHE COULD
HEAR MALGORN'S FOOTSTEPS AND DRACO'S GROWLS BEHIND HER.

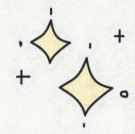

SHE FOUND A SMALL TUNNEL HIDDEN BETWEEN TWO SHELVES. SQUEEZING THROUGH, SHE ENTERED A SECRET ROOM FILLED WITH GLOWING SCROLLS.

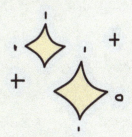

ELLIE OPENED THE BOOK. INSIDE WAS A MAP OF THE LIBRARY AND INSTRUCTIONS: ONLY A PURE HEART CAN UNLOCK ITS SECRETS.

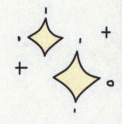

DRACO BURST INTO THE ROOM, PANTING. "MALGORN IS CLOSE.
DID YOU FIND ANYTHING?"
ELLIE SHOWED HIM THE MAP. "THIS MIGHT HELP!"

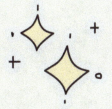

DRACO STUDIED IT QUICKLY. "THIS MARKS THE LIBRARY'S HEART—A PLACE WHERE MAGIC IS STRONGEST. WE MUST GET THERE BEFORE MALGORN!"

THE TUNNEL TREMBLED AS MALGORN'S VOICE ECHOED.
"YOU CAN'T HIDE FROM ME FOREVER!"

DRACO LOWERED HIS WING. "CLIMB ON!" HE SAID. ELLIE SCRAMBLED
ONTO HIS BACK AS DRACO SQUEEZED THROUGH THE TUNNEL.

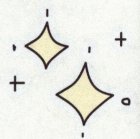

THEY EMERGED INTO A VAST CHAMBER FILLED WITH GLOWING CRYSTALS. IN THE CENTER STOOD A PEDESTAL HOLDING A SHIMMERING ORB.

"THE HEART OF THE LIBRARY," DRACO WHISPERED.
"THIS IS WHERE THE MAGIC FLOWS."

ELLIE SLID OFF DRACO'S BACK. "WHAT'S THE ORB FOR?" SHE ASKED, STARING AT THE PEDESTAL.

BEFORE DRACO COULD ANSWER, MALGORN APPEARED, HIS CLOAK BILLOWING. "YOU LED ME RIGHT TO IT. HOW KIND."

DRACO GROWLED, STEPPING PROTECTIVELY IN FRONT OF ELLIE.
"YOU WON'T TAKE THIS LIBRARY'S MAGIC!"

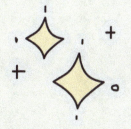

MALGORN LAUGHED. "OH, BUT I WILL. I'VE STUDIED THIS PLACE FOR YEARS. THE ORB IS THE KEY TO ULTIMATE POWER!"

ELLIE NOTICED RUNES CARVED AROUND THE PEDESTAL.
"DRACO, LOOK! THE RUNES MATCH THE BOOK!"

DRACO READ THE RUNES ALOUD. "TO PROTECT THE HEART, COURAGE AND KINDNESS MUST UNITE."

MALGORN RAISED HIS STAFF. "TOO LATE FOR RIDDLES!" HE SHOT A BLAST OF DARK ENERGY, BUT DRACO SHIELDED ELLIE WITH HIS WING.

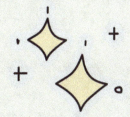

ELLIE GRABBED THE BOOK. "IT SAYS THE ORB RESPONDS TO PURE INTENTIONS."

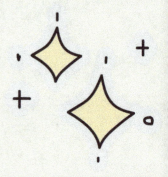

"THEN WE MUST ACT QUICKLY," DRACO SAID, HIS VOICE URGENT.
"TOUCH THE ORB, ELLIE."

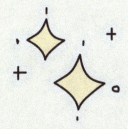

ELLIE HESITATED BUT STEPPED FORWARD. THE ORB GLOWED BRIGHTER AS SHE REACHED OUT, WARMTH SPREADING THROUGH HER FINGERTIPS.

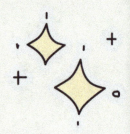

MALGORN ROARED. "NO! THAT POWER IS MINE!" HE LUNGED FOR ELLIE.

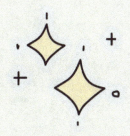

DRACO TACKLED MALGORN MID-AIR, SENDING THE WIZARD
CRASHING INTO THE GROUND.

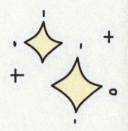

THE ORB PULSED WITH LIGHT, SURROUNDING ELLIE AND
DRACO IN A GOLDEN GLOW.

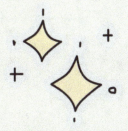

THE RUNES LIT UP, AND A PROTECTIVE BARRIER FORMED AROUND THE ORB.

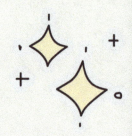

MALGORN SNARLED. "YOU CAN'T STOP ME!" HE SUMMONED
SHADOWS TO BREAK THE BARRIER.

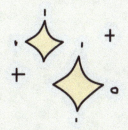

DRACO BREATHED FIRE, HOLDING THE SHADOWS AT BAY.
"ELLIE, KEEP GOING!"

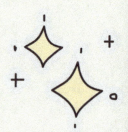

ELLIE CLOSED HER EYES, FOCUSING ON THE WARMTH OF THE ORB. "WE JUST WANT TO PROTECT THE LIBRARY," SHE WHISPERED.

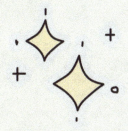

THE ORB RESPONDED, SENDING A BEAM OF LIGHT INTO THE CAVERN, PUSHING MALGORN BACK.

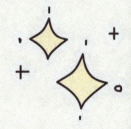

MALGORN SCREAMED AS THE LIGHT GREW BRIGHTER.
"THIS ISN'T OVER!" HE SHOUTED, VANISHING INTO THE SHADOWS.

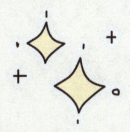

THE CAVERN STILLED. ELLIE OPENED HER EYES. "DID WE WIN?"

DRACO SMILED, HIS SCALES SHIMMERING IN THE GOLDEN GLOW.
"YOU DID IT, ELLIE. THE LIBRARY IS SAFE."

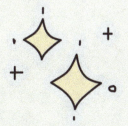

THE ORB FLOATED BACK TO ITS PEDESTAL, AND THE RUNES DIMMED.

ELLIE LOOKED AROUND. "WHAT HAPPENS NOW?"

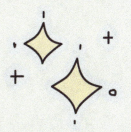

DRACO FOLDED HIS WINGS. "THE LIBRARY WILL REMAIN HIDDEN, BUT ITS MAGIC WILL ALWAYS PROTECT THOSE WITH PURE HEARTS."

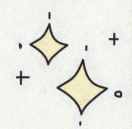

ELLIE BEAMED. "I'LL NEVER FORGET THIS PLACE."

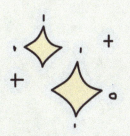

DRACO CHUCKLED. "AND THE LIBRARY WILL NEVER FORGET YOU."

AS THEY LEFT THE CHAMBER, THE CRYSTALS GLOWED SOFTLY,
AS IF SAYING GOODBYE.

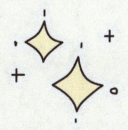

DRACO LED ELLIE BACK TO THE MAIN HALL. "YOUR COURAGE
SAVED THIS PLACE, ELLIE."

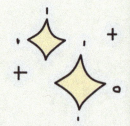

OUTSIDE THE LIBRARY, THE SNOWY FOREST
SPARKLED UNDER THE MOONLIGHT.

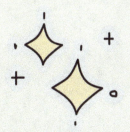

ELLIE LOOKED UP AT DRACO. "WILL I EVER SEE YOU AGAIN?"

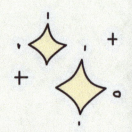

"Whenever you need me, just look for look for the library.

DRACO NODDED. "WHENEVER YOU NEED ME, JUST LOOK FOR THE LIBRARY."

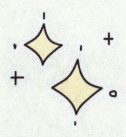

WITH ONE LAST SMILE, DRACO SPREAD HIS WINGS AND
SOARED INTO THE NIGHT.

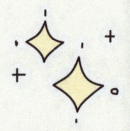

ELLIE STOOD IN THE CLEARING, CLUTCHING THE BOOK.
SHE FELT BRAVER THAN EVER.

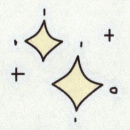

BACK HOME, ELLIE PLACED THE BOOK ON HER SHELF,
KNOWING ITS SECRETS WERE SAFE.

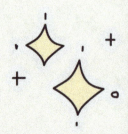

THE LIBRARY FADED BACK INTO LEGEND, HIDDEN FROM THE
WORLD BUT ALWAYS WAITING.

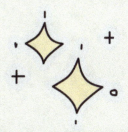

ELLIE TOLD NO ONE ABOUT HER ADVENTURE, BUT HER
HEART FELT LIGHTER WITH EACH DAY.

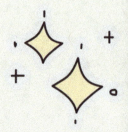

IN HER DREAMS, SHE OFTEN SAW DRACO FLYING
OVER THE SNOWY MOUNTAINS.

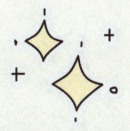

AND THOUGH THE LIBRARY WAS HIDDEN, ELLIE KNEW IT
WOULD ALWAYS BE THERE FOR THOSE WHO NEEDED IT.

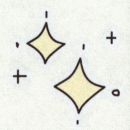

FAR AWAY, DRACO PERCHED ATOP A SNOWY PEAK, WATCHING OVER THE FOREST, THE LIBRARY, AND ITS BRAVE GUARDIAN.

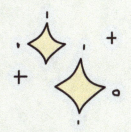

I HOPE YOU LIKED THE BOOK. PLEASE CHECK OUT MY OTHER BOOKS AND YOU CAN SEARCH MY AUTHOR NAME 'ROBY J JOHNSON'

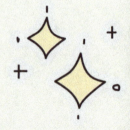